Florida-Backroads-Travel.com

CENTRAL WEST FLORIDA
BACKROADS TRAVEL

Second Edition, 2017

CONTENTS

Inverness ·
Homosassa Springs ·
CITRUS

· Brooksville
HERNANDO

Spring Hill ·
Hudson ·   · Dade City
PASCO

Port Richey ·
Tarpon Springs ·
PINELLAS   HILLSBOROUGH   · Plant City

Clearwater ·

· Tampa

St. Petersburg ·   · Ruskin

Bradenton ·   MANATEE

Sarasota ·
DESOTO
Arcadia ·

Venice ·   SARASOTA
North Port ·

Central
West

INTRODUCTION

Central West Florida Backroads Travel is your mentor through some of the most populated areas of the state. **Tampa, St. Petersburg, Clearwater, Bradenton** and **Sarasota** are major Florida towns in Central West Florida. You will also see some of the most rural and southern areas remaining in the state.

Central West Florida has 8 counties: **Citrus, Hernando, Pasco, Pinellas, Hillsborough, Manatee, Sarasota** and **DeSoto.**

All but Pinellas, Hillsborough and Sarasota counties are very rural. **Tampa, Orlando** and **Daytona Beach** are all growing toward each other along the **I-4 corridor** that connects east Florida to west Florida.

Culturally, Central West Florida is a composite of the other regions that make up Florida. The large cities have been populated over the years by northerners, primarily from the Midwest because of the major highways that come down the west coast of Florida from Indiana, Illinois, Ohio and Wisconsin. The rural counties are southern in culture. Here is where good old boys and Florida cowboys still roam much as they have for generations.

With **Busch Gardens, Florida Aquarium, Dali Museum** and other attractions in the region, and with Orlando only an hour or less away, this area is also a rival to Miami and Orlando in the Florida tourism industry.

The Central West Florida road map above will help you plan your trips.

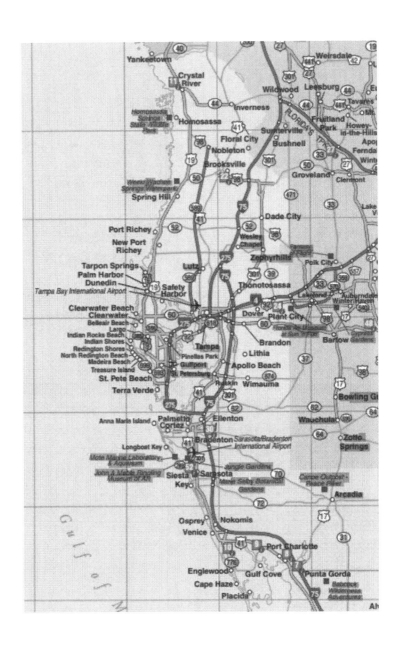

TOWNS AND CITIES

Central West Florida Backroads Travel lists places to stay and eat on many of the individual town pages. The individual pages include a brief history of the town along with my recommended motels, hotels and restaurants.

The towns and places in this guide include the following:

Arcadia

Bradenton

Cortez

Dade City

Englewood

Homosassa

Plant City

Sarasota

St Petersburg

Tampa

Venice

Arcadia

Arcadia is a town of about 7,000 people located in DeSoto County, Florida. It is located south of Wauchula at the intersection of US-17 and SR-70. Some historians say that a Reverend Hendry named the town in honor of Arcadia Albritton, a daughter of pioneer settlers who baked him a birthday cake.

This part of Florida is **cattle country**, although citrus and watermelons are important also. Cowboys are seen everywhere in Arcadia and the surrounding farms and villages. These aren't drug store cowboys; they are the real thing.

In the 1880's Arcadia Florida was the county seat of a very large county - DeSoto County - that would be broken into several smaller ones.

Bird's Eye View, Arcadia, Fla.

Charlotte, Hardee, Glades and **Highlands** Counties were broken out of DeSoto County, with Arcadia remaining the County Seat of DeSoto. These lands in the southeastern part of Central West

Florida have some of the most extensive cattle ranching operations in the state.

On **Thanksgiving Day 1905** Arcadia was nearly destroyed by a huge fire that burned down most of the business district. Most of the older buildings in town are dated from the years after that event.

In World War One, Arcadia was home to Carlstrom Field. It was used for pilot training then, and was also activated again for training World War Two pilots. Today the old base serves as the **Desoto County Juvenile Correctional Complex**. A plaque on the administration building memorializes the old Carlstrom Field. You can still see the outlines of the old airfields on aerial photographs of the area.

Arcadia is a **Florida Main Street** community, and has developed its downtown area into a pleasant location for antique shops, restaurants and mini-parks. Its cowboy heritage is also evident in the several rodeo events held each year. Nature lovers also enjoy paddling canoes down the Peace River.

ARCADIA RESTAURANTS

Magnolia Street Seafood and Grill, 9 W. Magnolia Street, Arcadia, FL 34266. 863-491-6916.

ARCADIA HOTELS

Oak Park Inn (bed and breakfast), 2 West Oak Street, Arcadia, FL 34266. 863 494-9500

Bradenton

Bradenton is located on US-41 between Tampa and Sarasota. It can also be entered from I-75 by exiting west on State Road 64. The population of Bradenton in the 2010 census was about 50,000.

Bradenton Florida History

Shaw's Point near Bradenton was discovered in 1539 by Hernando De Soto on one of his voyages to the New World.

The first town in the area was Manatee, incorporated in 1888. **Bradentown** was incorporated in 1903. It was named for Dr. **Joseph Braden** whose fortress-like house had been a refuge from settlers during Indian attacks.

The modern city of Bradenton Florida was formed in 1943, when the town of Manatee merged with Bradentown. The name of the new town became Bradenton, along with its new spelling.

Bradenton is surrounded by water, both fresh and salt. It is the access point for more than 20 miles of beautiful Florida beaches on the Gulf of Mexico and Tampa Bay. Bradenton is located on the mainland on the south bank of the Manatee River, and is separated from the outer barrier island beaches by the Intracoastal Waterway. These island beaches include **Anna Maria Island** and **Longboat Key**.

Old downtown Bradenton is located on the west side of the city.

Most of the office and government buildings in the county are located downtown. The tallest buildings in town are the 12 story Bradenton Financial Center and the new 9 story Manatee County Judicial Center. The new judicial center is right next to the historic courthouse.

Bradenton's downtown area is delightful and loaded with museums, restaurants and shops. It is a compact area, and everything is within an easy walk.

Just south of downtown is Bradenton's **Village of the Arts.** This is a neighborhood district with special zoning that allows residents to live and work in their homes. The creative zoning paid off. About 50 once rundown houses have been converted into studios, galleries, restaurants and other small businesses. The Village of The Arts has attracted national recognition because of its innovative approach.

Bradenton was recently recognized as one of the Top 10 cities in the country for working artists.

This award was made by Art Calendar, a well-known business magazine for visual artists.

BRADENTON RESTAURANTS

Pier 22 Restaurant. Indoor and outside dining on the waterfront. Good seafood and steaks, reasonably priced. 1200 1st Ave West, Bradenton, FL 34205. Tel: 941-748-8087.

Central Cafe Restaurant. Good salads and pizzas, full menu. 906 Manatee Ave East, Bradenton, FL 34208. Tel: 941-757-0050

BRADENTON HOTELS

Holiday Inn Express Bradenton West. This hotel is right downtown and is reasonably priced. 4450 47th St West, Bradenton, FL 34210. Tel: 941-795-4633.

The Londoner Bed and Breakfast. Very neat, clean and cozy in the heart of downtown. 304 15th Street West, Bradenton, **FL 34205. Tel: 941-748-5658.**

BRADENTON ATTRACTIONS

Manatee Players Riverfront Theater.. One of Florida's finest community theaters. The Manatee Players are an award winning troupe. 102 Old Main Street, Bradenton, FL 34205. Tel: 941-748-0111.

South Florida Museum. This is a one stop location for the museum, Bishop Planetarium and the Parker Manatee Aquarium. Location on Manatee River right downtown. 201 10th Street West, Bradenton, FL 34205. Tel: 941-746-4131

Art Center Manatee. Located in the heart of downtown, Art Center Manatee is Manatee County's premiere visual arts center. Nestled in the nearly 10,000 sq. ft. building are three galleries, five classrooms, an Artists' Market gift shop and an art library featuring over 3,000 art volumes. 209 9th Street West, Bradenton, FL 34205. Tel: 941-746-2862.

Cortez. This is a little commercial fishing village located between **Bradenton** and **Bradenton Beach**. Nice little bars and restaurants with fresh seafood. It's a quaint and scenic little working town.

Cortez

Cortez is a living remnant of **Old Florida**. It is a small working fishing village located on a peninsula in Sarasota Bay on Cortez Road (State Highway 684) that connects Bradenton and Bradenton Beach. It is not a trendy place, but a living community of weathered old houses and fish companies, fish nets, crab traps, floats and all kinds of boats, old and new.

It is fitting that several good seafood restaurants can be found in Cortez including Starfish Company, Cortez Kitchen, Swordfish Grill and Seafood Shack. These restaurants are able to serve fresh fish every day of the week, year round.

Cortez was founded about 1890 by several families from the waterfront town of Beaufort, North Carolina. These families are still represented in modern day Cortez. Some of the names are Guthrie, Bell, Taylor and Fulford.

This maritime heritage is showcased in The Florida Maritime Museum located in the restored 1912 school house at the

Cortez Nature Preserve. Cortez is also home to FISH (Florida Institute for Saltwater Heritage), a non-profit group set up in 1991 to help preserve the heritage of Florida Gulf Coast fishing communities.

Among events that also help preserve this heritage are the annual Cortez Commercial Fishing Festival, first held in 1981, and the recently initiated Ben Gullet Mullet Invitational.

The mullet event is a cast net only tournament that helps raise money for FISH and the Cortez Historical Society. It is named after the late **Ben Gullet** of Bradenton, who was well known as a cast net fisherman and mullet smoker (a man who cooks mullet in a smoker).

CORTEZ RESTAURANTS

Starfish Company Dockside Restaurant, 12306 46th Ave W, Cortez, FL 34215. 941-794-1243

CORTEZ HOTELS

Pelican Post Motel, 202 First St N., Bradenton Beach, FL 34217. 941-845-6253.

Dade City

Dade City is a small town of 6,500 people about 39 miles north of Tampa on U.S. Highway 301. It is the seat of Pasco County; the centerpiece of the historic downtown is the **Pasco County Courthouse**. In the 1870s there was a small town known as Fort Dade nearby. In the 1880s, the railroad bypassed Fort Dade a few miles to the east; the whole town packed up and moved to be next to the railroad. In 1884, the town was incorporated as Dade City.

Meridian St., Dade City, Fla.

The town is a popular destination for antique hunters; lots of antique shops, quaint restaurants and historic buildings are located downtown. Each year the town hosts the Kumquat Festival. The festival celebrates the kumquat, a tart citrus fruit that is grown all around the area. Another popular attraction is the Pioneer Florida Museum and Village on the east side of town.

This museum features all kinds of old farm equipment and antique tools used by the early pioneers in the area. A restored

1864 house is on the grounds, as well as an old railroad depot from the nearby town of Trilby. There is even an old locomotive on display. Detailed exhibits show how the early pioneers survived and prospered in the wilds of early Florida.

The Pasco County Courthouse was built in 1909 and has been restored a couple of times. It looks great, and is worth visiting just to take a look inside. The building is on The National Register of Historic Places.

A relatively new **Valentine's Day tradition** has been established in Dade City: the County Clerk performs a free wedding ceremony on the steps of the courthouse. What a great way for couples to remember their wedding anniversary date.

Other historic buildings in downtown Dade City include the Hugh Embry Library and the Edwinola Hotel; both structures are still in use today. Residential neighborhoods include many homes that were built in the Florida real estate boom of the 1920s.

A prisoner of war camp was located in Dade City during World War Two. The camp was for German soldiers who had been captured in North Africa as part of Field Marshal Erwin Rommel's Afrika Korp. The camp operated from 1942 to 1946. The camp is now repurposed as Pyracantha Park Civic Center.

DADE CITY RESTAURANTS

Rebecca's at City Market, 14148 8th Street, Dade City, Florida 33525. Tel: 352-521-9700

DADE CITY HOTELS

Hampton Inn Dade City-Zephyrhills, 13215 US HWY 301, Dade City, FL 33525. 855-271-3622

Englewood

Englewood is an unincorporated community that is partly in Sarasota County and partly in Charlotte County. About 16,000 people lived in the Englewood area in the year 2000. It's south of Venice on State Road 776. If you are heading south out of Venice on **US-41**, take **SR-776** due south right about the bend where US-41 turns to the east.

Until the late 1960's and early 1970's, Englewood was almost as quiet and out of the way as its southern neighbor, **Boca Grande**. Now old Englewood is surrounded by many developments, including two great big ones: **Northport** and **Rotonda.**

The first thing that happened to change Englewood's isolation was General Development's expansion of their Port Charlotte community northward from Charlotte County into Sarasota County. This expansion was initially called North Port Charlotte, and it was incorporated that way in 1959. Residents changed the name to North Port in 1974 so people wouldn't confuse it with Port Charlotte. Over 55,000 people now live in North Port.

The next big thing that happened was **Rotonda,** called Rotonda West by the Cavanagh Communities Corporation to differentiate it from Rotonda East they intended to develop on the east coast in southern Martin County and northern Palm Beach County. Rotonda East never happened, but Rotonda West now has nearly 8,000 people scattered around its uniquely circular layout. Cavanagh Communities went broke some time ago, but there are many thousands of lots still available for homes.

Once you get past these sprawling communities with thousands of scattered homes of standard Florida design dating from the 1960's to modern times, you get into Englewood Florida proper. It is a typical old Florida town nestled along the shores of Lemon Bay, an estuary of the Gulf of Mexico. The old part of town is centered along West Dearborn Street west of SR-776, also known as Indiana Avenue in this area.

The downtown area is nicely painted with plenty of pastel colors and a nice mural here and there. It is not a fancy gentrified area, but a real working village. There are many nice shops and several neat little restaurants with plenty of outside dining.

The town has a dry storage marina with a few boat slips among many older and modern neighborhoods with canals and boat slips. **Manasota Key** is located across Lemon Bay from Englewood, and is an easy drive for a day at the beach. Englewood is a pleasant place to while away a day or a week.

ENGLEWOOD RESTAURANTS

Mango Bistro, 301 W. Dearborn St., Englewood, Florida 34223. Tel: 941-681-3500

ENGLEWOOD HOTELS

Pearl Beach Inn, 7990 Manasota Key Road, Englewood, Florida 34223. Tel: 941-451-5284

Homosassa

Homosassa is in far northern Central West Florida near Weeki Wachee springs. Both places are examples of Old Florida. There are not many places left in sunny Florida that can give you a glimpse of the past. This little town nestles on the banks of the Crystal River about an hour north of St. Pete and Clearwater just off U.S. Highway 19.

You don't need an agenda to enjoy Homosassa, but there are still quite a few things to do if you get bored of soaking up the sleepy southern ambiance. **Manatee watching** is a favorite activity up here, along with fishing.

Homosassa Springs State Wildlife Park is a place where a pontoon boat will take you on a lazy trip up the **Homosassa River**. You will see Florida as it used to be but is rarely seen today. Along the way you can see the **Manatee Education Center**. It's a recovery facility for injured manatees. You might get to see deer, bear, bobcats and many birds, all in their natural settings.

The Yulee Sugar Mill State Park is the site of an old 5,100 acre sugar mill, which was used to supply troops during the Civil War. The park is named after Florida's first Jewish U.S. Senator, **David Levy Yulee**.

Scalloping in Homosassa is a popular annual phenomenon that draws thousands of happy hunters to the area. The scalloping season starts June 27 and runs through September 24. With a mask, snorkel and fins you can float along the shallow gulf waters and harvest your limit of the tasty creatures.

There are also a few nice places in Homosassa where you can sit and watch the river roll slowly by and think back on a simpler time in Florida.

HOMOSASSA RESTAURANTS

The Freezer, 5590 S Boulevard, Homosassa, FL 34446. Tel: 352-628-2452

HOMOSASSA HOTELS

Homosassa River Retreat, 10605 Hall's River Rd, Homosassa, FL 34446. Tel: 352-628-7072

Plant City

Plant City is a small town between Lakeland and Tampa. More than 75 percent of the winter strawberries in the United States come from Plant City. The town is grateful for its strawberry bounty, and celebrates every spring with the **Florida Strawberry Festival**. This festival is very popular and ranks in the Top 40 of all fairs in North America. It's a great opportunity to visit Plant City and see what one small town has done to preserve and celebrate its history.

Many people assume that Plant City got its name from its agricultural activities. Actually, the town is named for **Henry Plant**, a railroad pioneer who did for central and west Florida what **Henry Flagler** did for Florida's east coast.

In the 1880s, Plant bought railroads and extended them into then undeveloped Florida, opening up the area to agriculture including not just strawberries, but blueberries, citrus and whatever the Florida soil could produce.

Plant's railroads made it possible for Florida farmers to ship their products directly and cheaply to northern markets. Plant's railroad came to Plant City in 1884, and the community was immediately named for him.

The railroad's contribution to the community is celebrated in a lovely new museum in downtown Plant City.

Another amazing feature of the downtown area is the statuary. For example, the soldier and the woman greeting him at the station are realistic statues.

Statues of people in various poses are strategically placed throughout downtown. They give you the feeling that you are not alone. Even if there are few real people on the streets, you will still feel like you are one person of many. When I first saw the statue of the man sleeping, I thought he was real. After I took the photo I got closer to him and realized he was a life-like statue.

Plant City's downtown area is a great place to visit. There are many gift shops and antique stores and quite a few good restaurants. It's easy to spend an entire day just browsing the numerous shops.

The community has done a wonderful job sprucing up and restoring old buildings that are being put to good use today.

Even the old Plant City High School, built in 1914, is still standing and is in pretty good condition.

PLANT CITY RESTAURANTS

Krazy Kup, 101 E J Arden Mays Blvd, Plant City, FL 33563. Tel: 813-752-1220

PLANT CITY HOTELS

Holiday Inn Express, 2102 N Park Rd, Plant City, FL 33566. Tel: (813) 719-3800

Sarasota

Sarasota, like many places in the state, was originally the home of Native Americans who began settling in the area about 10,000 years ago. The first Europeans to discover the area were the Spanish, who landed at Charlotte Harbor to the south in 1513.

Sarasota Bay is large and sheltered from the Gulf of Mexico by barrier islands. The bay became a seasonal place for fishing and trading by Americans and Cubans in the years leading up to Florida becoming a United States territory in 1821.

White settlers began moving into the area in big numbers by the 1840's. The area was known by then as **Zara Zote** on old Spanish maps, and the newcomers began calling the area Sara Sota.

William Whitaker was reportedly the first permanent resident of what became in later years the City of Sarasota Florida. He sold fish and raised cattle, and married Mary Jane Wyatt of Manatee and they had 11 children. This family survived many hardships of pioneer life, including raids by the Seminole Indians. Many descendants of this family still live in Sarasota.

Sarasota was incorporated in the early 1900's. One of the earliest developers was **Owen Burns**, who built many buildings, houses, roads and bridges. **John Ringling** of circus fame was one of his earliest investors, but Burns went broke anyway in the depression that ended the big Florida land boom of the 1920's. Ringling went broke not long after.

A contemporary of Burns that had a huge impact on Sarasota was **Mrs. Potter Palmer**. Born Bertha Honore', she married Chicago millionaire Potter Palmer when she was 21 and he was 44. Bertha liked to spend money, but she also proved to be an excellent businesswoman. When her husband died in 1902, she took over his business interests. She loved the mild winter climate of Sarasota, and bought more than 80,000 acres of land in the area in 1910. She bought another 19,000 acres in 1914 in the Temple Terrace area east of Tampa.

Mrs. Palmer became a big time land developer, banker, cattle rancher, citrus farmer and Florida socialite. She encouraged many of her rich friends to spend their winters in Sarasota. Some of the land she owned is still known today as **Palmer Ranch**, one of Florida's largest planned communities. **Palmer Bank** was one of the most important banks in Sarasota until it merged with Southeast Banks in 1976.

Mrs. Palmer died in 1918. In the 16 years after her husband's death, she more than doubled the family fortune. Her sons continued to operate the family empire. They eventually transferred their huge cattle ranch, **Meadowsweet Pastures**, to the State of Florida. It became **Myakka River State Park**.

During Mrs. Palmer's time in Sarasota, she drew worldwide recognition for the city as an exclusive vacation destination and location for winter homes for wealthy northerners. Among these were **John and Mable Ringling**, and John's brother Charles.

John and Mable built their magnificent mansion, **Ca d'Zan** (House of John) in 1925, and today it is an art museum on the National Register of Historic Places. Charles's estate became the campus of New College. Both Ringlings were active in the development of Sarasota, and in the cultural affairs of the community. Like many Floridians, they lost most of their fortunes in the collapse of the 1920's land boom.

When John Ringling died in 1936, he had less than $400 in his bank account.

These pioneers had much to do with what Sarasota has become today. The opera, theaters, ballet performances, museums, art museums and schools were all grown from the seeds planted by the early visionaries. The **Florida West Coast Symphony**, **Ringling School of Art** and **Asolo Theatre Company** were all or in part gifts of wealthy benefactors.

When these cultural amenities are combined with the natural ones like Gulf sunsets, boating from many marinas including **Marina Jack** right downtown, tropical landscaping, shell collecting, bird watching, balmy winter weather and well-designed golf courses, Sarasota is a great place to visit or live.

Probably more than any other place in Florida, the blue green waters of the Gulf of Mexico against the backdrop of sparkling white beaches make you feel like you are in a tropical paradise.

SARASOTA RESTAURANTS

Marina Jack, 2 Marina Plaza, Sarasota, Florida 34236. Tel: 941-365-4232.

SARASOTA HOTELS

Coquina on the Beach, 1008 Ben Franklin Drive, Sarasota, Florida 34236. Tel: 941-306-2256.

St Petersburg

St Petersburg is called St Pete by most natives of the Tampa Bay area. The population is about 250,000. St Pete is within the Tampa Bay Metropolitan Statistical area of about 2.7 million residents.

History of St Petersburg

The city had two major founders: **John C. Williams** of Detroit, who bought the land that is now St Pete in 1876, and **Peter Demens**, a Russian who was instrumental in bringing the terminus of the railroad there in 1888. St Petersburg was incorporated in 1892 with a population of only about 300 people. Demens named it after his former hometown of St Petersburg Russia.

St Pete is located on a large peninsula between Tampa Bay and the Gulf of Mexico. The peninsula is surrounded by some of the prettiest waters in Florida.

This peninsular location isolated St Pete from the rest of Florida in its early days. In the early 1900's a channel was dredged out into Tampa Bay and this made St Petersburg became a significant port city. It was still a long way from anywhere by land, however. It was a winding 43 mile trip from St Pete to Tampa through Oldsmar on the north side of the bay.

The first commercial airline service was started in 1914 with a seaplane. It was known as the St Petersburg–Tampa Airboat Line. The first pilot was **Tony Jannus**. Jannus Landing, a local music and entertainment venue on Central Avenue in downtown St Pete is named in his honor.

Promoter **George Gandy** built the first bridge over Tampa Bay in 1924. At last, St Petersburg was a convenient trip to and from Tampa. The other bridge that connects St Pete to Tampa is the **Howard Frankland Bridge** that carries **I-275** from North St Pete to west Tampa.

In the years after World War Two, St Pete became a mecca for retired people. They flocked to the sunshine and lived in the many residential hotels in the downtown area. The symbol of St Pete became old people sitting on the many **green benches** that dotted the sidewalks of the city.

St Petersburg Today

Today's downtown St Petersburg has marinas brimming with hundreds of sailboats and almost as many power boats. Tampa Bay is great sailing territory. There is a significant marine industry in town. Unlike the rest of Florida, a few of the boatyards have not been converted to condominiums or marinas.

St Petersburg has long been nicknamed **The Sunshine City**, and was a retirement location for northerners. When I first moved to Florida in 1960, St Pete was known as **"God's Waiting Room"**, and the streets were lined with green park benches upon which were perched thousands of old timers watching the world go by.

The **St Petersburg Pier** has been the centerpiece of downtown for years. Demolition is underway in 2015 and the pier will be replaced by a futuristic new structure sometime in 2017.

To paraphrase a popular car commercial of some years ago, this ain't your father's St Pete.

The old apartment and condo buildings of "God's Waiting Room" of 50 years ago have been either torn down or renovated. Old homes have been purchased and restored. The entire downtown area is vibrant and alive, night and day. My favorite place to stay downtown is the **Renaissance Vinoy**

Hotel, a beautifully restored structure on the **National Register of Historic Places**.

THINGS TO DO IN ST PETERSBURG

St Pete's downtown has many walkable attractions. A children's museum, a museum of fine arts, a history museum, a Holocaust Museum, and the **Salvador Dalí Museum,** which houses the largest collection of original Dalí's outside of Europe. There are dozens of smaller art galleries, small entertainment clubs, theaters, and a massive waterfront park system that showcases the marinas and the legendary St. Petersburg Pier, a popular Florida tourist attraction.

The pier contains a small aquarium open to the public, retail shopping, adventure activities, and both casual and fine dining restaurants. Various sightseeing boat rides are also offered.

The Bounty II, a replica of HMS Bounty used in the 1962 MGM movie starring Marlon Brando was permanently docked near the Pier for many years until the ship was sold in 1986. Now it only comes to St Pete for the winter. If you want to see the Pier, do it soon. It is scheduled to be demolished in the near future.

The **BayWalk** shopping complex is also downtown, with an IMAX Muvico 20 screen movie theater, as well as many chain restaurants and retail shops. The University of South Florida St Petersburg Florida campus is also downtown.

Every Saturday morning, from October to May, the downtown area hosts a **farmers market** in the parking area of Al Lang Field (now also known as Progress Energy Park). Local vendors sell produce, vegetables, fruit, arts and crafts in a festive atmosphere.

The **Grand Central** district, part of historic Kenwood, is due west of downtown St Pete on Central Avenue. It has a vibrant artistic community that contributes to the ambiance of downtown St Pete.

Tropicana Field, home of Major League Baseball's **Tampa Bay Rays** is also located in the western part of downtown.

St Petersburg Florida is just a short drive from the Gulf beaches of St Pete Beach, Pass-A-Grille and others. Fort Desoto State Park has a beach that Dr. Beach has ranked number one in the USA.

South of St Pete, the peninsula is connected to the south side of Tampa Bay near Palmetto and Bradenton by the modern Sunshine Skyway Bridge that carries I-275. The view from this bridge is one of the most magnificent in Florida.

ST PETE RESTAURANTS

Chattaway, 358 22nd Ave S, St. Petersburg, Florida 33705. Tel: 727-823-1594. Close to downtown with great outside dining in an artistic eclectic atmosphere. Famous burger and other good stuff too.

ST PETE HOTELS

Beach Drive Inn Bed & Breakfast, 532 Beach Drive NE, St. Petersburg, FL 33701. Tel: 727-822-2244. An elegant Key West Style house built in 1910 and restored in 2007. This historic inn is located in the charming downtown waterfront district of St. Petersburg near the Renaissance Vinoy Hotel. It is within a short walk of St. Pete's finest attractions including the Bayside Beach, Vinoy Park and Jannus landing, the Pier, Baywalk, museums, and restaurants. It is on the National Register of Historic Places.

Renaissance Vinoy Resort & Golf Club, 501 5th Avenue NE, St. Petersburg, FL 33701. Tel: 727-894-1000. I stayed here, and it is an amazing place. The resort includes a private marina, 18-hole golf course and 12-court tennis complex. The large hotel has been beautifully restored to its 1920's elegance. It is a classic example of Mediterranean Revival architecture, and it is on the National Register of Historic Places. It is within easy walking distance of all of downtown St. Pete's attractions. It is a typically well maintained Marriott property with a knowledgeable and friendly staff.

Tampa

The modern history of Tampa began when Spanish explo
visited the area in the 1520's. After the Spanish left, the Tampa
area was sparsely settled for the next couple of hundred years.
During the Seminole Wars in Florida, the U.S. built a series of
forts and trading posts. Fort Brooke was established at the
mouth of the Hillsborough River near today's downtown Tampa
Convention Center. It became the first real settlement in Tampa
history.

Tampa suffered at Union hands during the Civil War. Florida was
a Confederate state and the Union navy set up a blockade
around Tampa. The Union finally occupied the city after the war
was over, and stayed there until 1869. The Reconstruction
period after the Civil War was very a very hard time in Tampa
history. There was no industry and very poor roads to and from
the rest of the state. Throughout Tampa history, the area had
been affected by yellow fever epidemics borne by mosquitoes
from the surrounding swampland, but the sickness was
particularly widespread during the late 1860s and 1870s.

Tampa's modern history began to develop when Henry Plant
brought the railroad to town in 1885. The railroad link attracted
the cigar industry. **Vicente Martinez Ybor** moved his cigar
manufacturing operations to Tampa from Key West. Nearness
to Cuba made imports of tobacco easy by sea, and Plant's
railroad made shipment of finished cigars to the rest of the US
market easy by land.

Ybor built hundreds of small houses around his factory to
accommodate the immediate influx of mainly Cuban and
Spanish cigar workers. His factory and housing development
were known as Ybor City, a place still famous in Tampa history.

Other cigar factories soon moved in, and Ybor City quickly made Tampa a major cigar production center.

Many Italian and a few eastern European Jewish immigrants also arrived starting in the late 1880s, operating businesses and shops that catered to the cigar workers. The majority of Italian immigrants came from Alessandria Della Rocca and Santo Stefano Quisquina, two small Sicilian towns with which Tampa still maintains strong ties.

In 1891, Henry B. Plant built a lavish 500 room , Moorish Revival style luxury resort hotel called the **Tampa Bay Hotel** on 150 landscaped acres along the Hillsborough River. The massive structure cost $2.5 million to build.

Plant filled his expensive hotel with exotic art collectibles from around the world and installed electric lights and the first elevator in Tampa. The resort did well for a few years, especially during the Spanish-American War. Teddy Roosevelt and his famous Rough Riders were among the 30,000 troops housed in the hotel during the war.

With Plant's death in 1899, the hotel's fortunes began to fade. It closed in 1930. In 1933 the stately building reopened as the University of Tampa.

During the first few decades of the 20th century, the cigar making industry was the backbone of Tampa's economy. The factories in Ybor City and West Tampa made huge numbers of cigars. In the peak year of 1929, over 500,000,000 cigars were hand rolled in Tampa.

In 1904, a local civic association of local businessmen dubbed themselves Ye Mystic Krewe of Gasparilla (named after mythical pirate Jose Gaspar), and staged an "invasion" of the city followed by a parade. Jose Gaspar supposedly lived on nearby Gasparilla Island. Ye Mystic Krewe continues to exist today, and is a prestigious community involvement group that enjoys tremendous support from the people of Tampa. With a few exceptions, the **Gasparilla Pirate Festival** has been held every year since, and is a large part of the celebration of Tampa history.

Tampa began to boom during and after World War II. **MacDill Field** was built as a main base of operations for the United States Army Air Force, along with auxiliary fields in north Tampa and north St. Petersburg. At the end of the war, MacDill remained as an active military installation while the auxiliary fields reverted to civilian control.

Two of these auxiliary fields would later become the present day **Tampa International Airport** (from the old Drew Field) and **St. Petersburg-Clearwater International Airport**. The **Tampa**

Bay Bucs of the NFL play in the modern Raymond James Stadium just east of Tampa International Airport.

Tampa is still one of Florida's most diverse cities, reflecting its earlier Hispanic and Italian heritage. Modern Tampa is a city of neighborhoods, many of them originally inhabited by various ethnic and cultural groups. A few of these neighborhoods close to downtown are:

Hyde Park, near downtown on the west side of the Hillsborough River. It has been renovated in recent years to create trendy housing, restaurants and shopping.

Ballast Point, **Bayshore, Palma Ceia** and **Westshore** are old neighborhoods with fine large homes north of MacDill Air Force Base.

Davis Islands is a 1920's boom town development dredged up from Tampa Bay immediately south of downtown.

Harbour Island is immediately south of the heart of downtown Tampa. It was originally known as Seddon Island, and not to many years ago it was a seedy rundown industrial port. In 1979 it was purchased from the railroad, and redeveloped into today's fine condominiums, marinas, shops, offices and restaurants.

Like most Florida cities, Tampa has sprawled out from its center and is now surrounded by many beautiful suburbs and new towns. **Sun City**, for example, is south of Tampa and is one of the largest Florida active retirement communities.

Most areas of Tampa are safe, but like all big cities it's best to have some local advice before wandering around in some places and neighborhoods you don't know anything about. Tampa is also a good place to start and finish one of your favorite Florida day trips.

Its central location on the Gulf coast means there are many opportunities for one tank trips not only in Central West Florida, but in Southwest and Central Florida also.

TAMPA HOTELS

Holiday Inn Express. This is a new motel, very clean and reasonably priced on the north side of town in New Tampa. Free breakfast and very kid friendly. 8310 Galbraith Road (I-75 (exit 270) @ Bruce B. Downs Blvd., Tampa Fla 33647. Tel: 1-800-423-0908.

Spring Hill Suites Tampa Brandon. This motel is in the Brandon area of Tampa, east of downtown. Nice and clean and convenient. 1051 S. Falkenburg Road, Tampa Fla 33619. Tel: 813-623-9990.

Palmer House Bed and Breakfast, 2221 Hinton Ranch Road, Lithia, FL 33547. The Palmer House Bed and Breakfast has a country feeling, yet it is close to Tampa and Orlando. A great place for a Florida getaway weekend. Relaxing, horseback riding, canoeing on the Alafia River. Easy drive to Tampa. Southern hospitality. Hot tub, oak trees, bench swing.

TAMPA RESTAURANTS

Bern's Steak House. I first had dinner at Bern's in 1968, and still consider it to be one of the best steak houses in Florida. The place has great service and quality food, much of it grown on their own farm. They have an extensive menu and wine list. The dessert room upstairs is a treat and not to be missed. 1208 South Howard Avenue, Tampa Fla 33606. Tel: 813-251-2421.

The Columbia Restaurant. The Columbia is as much an Ybor City tourist attraction as it is a fine restaurant. The ambience is vintage Cuban and Spanish, with lots of arches and Spanish tile. As far as I know, the Columbia has been open continuously since 1905. They have many Cuban dishes like fried plantains, beans, tostones, yucca and rice. Their seafood is also wonderful. In addition to the good food, they have a live floor show with attractive and talented Spanish flamenco dancers. 2117 E 7TH Ave, Tampa Fla 33605-3903. Tel: 813-248-4961.

Saigon Bay Vietnamese Restaurant. Delicious and authentic Vietnamese food. They have the usual Pho noodle soup, bun bo nuong, many lightly stir fried entrees. The food is very healthy, similar to Thai cuisine. They focus on seafood here, and their Com Xao Cua (crab fried rice) is great. Prices are very reasonable. 2373 E Fowler Ave, Tampa, Fla 33612-5509. Tel: 813-971-0854.

TAMPA ATTRACTIONS

Busch Gardens. This was one of the first major theme parks in modern Florida, having opened in 1959. It originally opened as a bird garden and hospitality center with free beer to guests who toured the Anheuser-Busch Brewery. It has been continuously updated, and is still a fun place to visit. It has a world class zoo with more than 2500 animals, and a bunch of excellent roller coasters. 10165 N McKinley Drive, Tampa, Florida 33612. Tel: 1-888-800-5447.

The Florida Aquarium. This Tampa aquarium is one of the top aquariums in the world. It features more than 20,000 aquatic plants and animals from Florida and around the world! The Florida Aquarium's 2-acre outdoor water adventure zone lets the kids cool off while parents relax under the shade of the Tampa Tribune Cantina bar and grill with a good view of the play area. Daily Hours: 9:30 AM to 5:00 PM, closed on Thanksgiving and Christmas. 701 Channelside Drive, Tampa, Florida 33602. Tel: 813-273-4000

The Ybor City Museum. This is a state historic park consisting of the Ybor City Museum, housed in the Ferlita Bakery building, the Casita, and the Garden. The park contains permanent exhibits on Vicente Martinez Ybor, the founding and early history of Ybor City, the cigar industry, the social clubs of the city, and the Ferlita Bakery itself. The Casita is actually one of seven small cottages, built for cigar workers' families that are located at this historic site. The Garden is a version of the Mediterranean-style patios seen in the late 19th century. 1818 East 9th Avenue, Tampa, Florida 33605. Tel: 813-247-6323.

Venice

Venice began when an early pioneer, Richard Roberts established a homestead in the 1870's near Roberts Bay and the beach. He planted an orange grove and a few other crops. The area supported a few citrus operations, along with boat building and fishing until the turn of the century. The early settlers chose the name Venice for their community post office. It was located south of **Shakett Creek** on what is now Portia Street in Nokomis. Modern Venice is about 25 miles south of Sarasota.

The railroad came to Sarasota County in 1911, and development followed in the path of the rails. **Mrs. Potter Palmer,** a wealthy Chicago woman, bought 60,000 acres in Sarasota County. Her land development operation platted an area south of Robert's Bay and called it Venice. The rails were extended to the new village of Venice. The new little town began to grow slowly, but it remained a small citrus and fishing community until the 1920's Florida land boom.

In 1925, **Dr. Fred H. Albee**, a prosperous orthopedic surgeon, purchased 2,916 acres of land from Mrs. Palmer. He hired **John Nolan**, a city planner, to design a city on his land. Dr. Albee's dream was to cure sick patients using the magic power of sunshine. It's obvious he was not a dermatologist.

Before he started on his plan, however, he sold the land to the **Brotherhood of Locomotive Engineers**, a labor union. They made him an offer he couldn't refuse. The union organized **BLE Realty Corporation** to develop the property. The main feature of the development plan was **Venice Avenue**, a 200 foot wide boulevard terminating at the Gulf of Mexico beach. Construction got underway and the town began to emerge from the palmettos and sand dunes. The **Hotel Venice** opened in 1926. It had 100 rooms with private baths, and was magnificent for its time.

There were very few Florida towns like Venice back then. That remains true today. This was one of the first places in the state that had strict zoning regulations and design review requirements. All buildings had to be constructed in the Northern Italian Renaissance style. Roof lines and tiles, awnings, building colors, relationships to adjacent buildings and setbacks were all carefully regulated. The result is the friendly ambiance of today's downtown Venice.

The great depression devastated Venice, and the economic fallout from the great Miami hurricanes of 1926 and 1928 finished the job. Venice languished in a severe depression until World War Two. Before the war, Dr. Albee bought a hotel and converted it to Florida Medical Center. It specialized in heliotropic healing: using the sun to heal.

The Venice Army Air Base was built on land south of town during the war, and brought much needed jobs and activity to the area.

The City of Venice obtained the air base after the war, and it is still in use today as a general aviation airport.

I've always been fond of Venice. My grandparents retired to this area in 1960. They lived in Nokomis, a little village north of town. They rented a little two bedroom terrazzo floored house with no air conditioning for $ 75 per month. That ate up most of their retirement income, so they worked at odd jobs around town. Grandpa actually died on the job as a substitute gym teacher.

The Ringling Brothers Barnum and Baily circus moved their winter quarters to Venice in 1960. My grandparents loved going to the quarters and watching the performers and animals rehearse.

Venice today is still a pedestrian friendly little town that has it all. Good shopping, restaurants, art, boating, beaches and walking. Many people think that Venice has the best beaches in Florida.

The main thoroughfare of Venice is US-41, the Tamiami Trail, that runs generally north and south through town on its way from Tampa to Miami.

The heart of the town, however, lies along **West Venice Avenue** and the surrounding historic district. This broad boulevard is lined with charming sidewalk cafes and unique boutiques. It is a shopper's paradise. Several great antique shops are located on **"Antique Row"** along Miami Avenue one block south of Venice Avenue. The town also has its own live theater and symphony orchestra.

Venice has beautiful natural beaches, and is known as the **"Shark Tooth Capital Of The World"**. Needless to say, you can find a few of these teeth along the beach. Don't be alarmed. These are from sharks that died hundreds of thousands of years ago.

Head north from Venice to Nokomis and drive out to Casey Key. Go north along the Gulf. The narrow road is shaded under canopies of tropical trees, and the blue water of the Gulf glistens over your left shoulder.

This drive will take you north for several miles to **Blackburn Point Road** where you will return to the mainland at **Osprey**. Leave your windows open and enjoy the sea breeze.

VENICE RESTAURANTS

It's best to make reservations at Venice restaurants in season, say **December through March.**

Cafe Venice. In the heart of historic downtown Venice. Good seafood, nice bar, outside dining. 116 W Venice Ave, Venice Fla. Tel: 941-484-1855.

Cassariano Italian Eatery. Good Italian pasta and seafood dishes. Right downtown in the historic district. 313 West Venice Avenue, Venice. Tel: 941-485-0507.

VENICE HOTELS

Floridaloha Vacations. These unique cottages are near everything in Venice and are all decorated in an Old Florida theme. You can select from one of three cottages. 202 E. Pocono Trail, Nokomis, Florida 34275. Tel: 941-375-4499.

Venice Beach Villas. Efficiencies, studios, and one or two bedroom units for the family. Nice clean facility near family beaches. 501 W. Venice Avenue, Venice Florida. Tel: 941-488-1580.

Horse and Chaise Inn, 317 Ponce de Leon, Venice Florida 34285. Tel: 941-488-2702. This bed and breakfast is in the heart of historic old downtown. Nice, comfortable and clean with friendly hosts who are longtime residents.

VENICE ATTRACTIONS

Venice Theatre. Since 1998, Venice Theatre has received more awards than any other community theatre in Florida and in the Southeastern United States. 140 West Tampa Ave, Venice. 941-488-1115.

Venice Art Center. The oldest and largest community art center on Florida's Southwest coast. Art classes, workshops, summer camps, and ongoing exhibits. Open from 9am to 4pm daily. 390 S. Nokomis Avenue, Venice. Tel: 941-485-7136.

Shelling On The Beaches. If my grandmother were still alive she would want me to tell you that the best thing to do in Venice is go to the beach. Sift through the beach sand for beautiful shells and shark teeth. She liked the beach on Casey Key the best of all.

BEACHES

Central West Florida Travel Guide will show you of the best beaches in Florida. Many of them are covered on the individual town pages and are in **Bradenton Beach, Englewood, Sarasota,** the **St Pete beach towns** and **Venice.**

The beaches in Central West Florida are magnificent and sandy from Venice in the south up to Caladesi Island north of Dunedin. The Gulf of Mexico is usually warmer and calmer than the Atlantic.

The only **downside** is that the Florida Gulf Coast is troubled once in a while by **"red tide"**. This is a form of floating algae bloom that kills fish and makes your eyes water. It won't kill you, but you won't enjoy it. You also won't want to spend much time at the beach if the red tide is too close off shore. If it happens, it is usually in the summer but not always.

The Florida Fish and Wildlife Conservation Commission website (**myfwc.com/REDTIDESTATUS**) will tell you the status of red tide currents. Don't book any beach time if you learn the red tide is around. Many Florida travel brochures and websites won't warn you about this. It's a minor problem, but a problem nonetheless. Red tide has been documented in these waters since the 1700s; it's not a new problem.

Some of our favorite beaches in this region, from north to south, are:

Caladesi Island State Park, Dunedin. Untouched stretches of beautiful white sand beach. Accessible by boat. Camping and day tripping.

Clearwater Beach, on the same barrier island as Caladesi Island State Park.

The St Pete Beaches, the small communities from **Clearwater** on the north to **Pass A Grille** on the south. Includes **Indian Rocks Beach**, **Indian Shores, Redington Beach**, **Madeira Beach**, **Treasure Island**, **St. Pete Beach** and **Pass A Grille**. Miles and miles of beautiful beaches and reasonable places to stay.

Fort DeSoto Park, Tierra Verde. Beautiful sand beaches open to the public along with a lot of natural attractions in a public park. The park is at the entrance to Tampa Bay.

The Gulf Beaches, from **Anna Maria** to **Venice** including **Longboat Key, Siesta Key** and **Venice**. Many miles of easily accessible and beautiful white sand – or shell in some cases – beaches.

Casey Key, Venice. One of many beaches on the barrier island off the coast of Venice.

STATE PARKS

There are 27 beautiful state parks in Central West Florida offering a variety of experiences including camping, boating, beaching and hiking. There is something for everyone. Your Florida travel experience will be enhanced by visiting one of our beautiful state parks.

Here are addresses and telephone numbers for Central West Florida State Parks. The parks that I've listed in **BOLD PRINT CAPITAL LETTERS** have full service campgrounds.

Some of the others may have no camping at all, or primitive, equestrian or group camping.

> **ALAFIA RIVER STATE PARK**, 14326 South County Road 39, Lithia, FL 33547 813-672-5320
>
> Anclote Key Preserve State Park, # 1 Causeway Blvd., Dunedin, FL 34698 727- 469-5942
>
> Caladesi Island State Park, # 1 Causeway Blvd., Dunedin, FL 34698 727-469-5918
>
> Crystal River Preserve State Park, 3266 North Sailboat Avenue Crystal River, Florida 34428. Tel: 352-563-0450
>
> Cayo Costa State Park, P.O. Box 1150, Boca Grande, FL 33921 941-964-0375
>
> Colt Creek State Park, 16000 State Rd 471, Lakeland, FL 33809. 863-815-6761
>
> Crystal River Archaeological State Park 3400 N. Museum Point Crystal River, Florida 34428. Tel: 352-795-3817

Crystal River Preserve State Park, 3266 North Sailboat Avenue, Crystal River, Florida 34428. Tel: 352-563-0450

Dade Battlefield Historic State Park, 7200 CR 603 South Battlefield Drive, Bushnell, FL 33513. 352-793-4781

Don Pedro Island State Park, P.O. Box 1150, Boca Grande, FL 33921. 941-964-0375

Egmont Key State Park, 4905 34th Street South, #5000, St. Petersburg, FL 33711. 727-893-2627

Fort Cooper State Park, 3100 South Old Floral City Road, Inverness, FL 34450. 352-726-0315

Fort Foster Historic Site, Hillsborough River State Park, 15402 US 301 North, Thonotosassa, FL 33592. 813-987-6771

Gamble Plantation Historic State Park, 3708 Patten Avenue, Ellenton, FL 34222. 941-723-4536

Gasparilla Island State Park, P.O. Box 1150, Boca Grande, FL 33921. 941-964-0375

HILLSBOROUGH RIVER STATE PARK, 15402 U.S. 301 N., Thonotosassa, FL 33592. 813-987-6771

Homosassa Springs Wildlife State Park, 4150 S. Suncoast Blvd., Homosassa, Florida 34446. Tel: 352-628-5343

Honeymoon Island State Park, 1 Causeway Blvd., Dunedin, FL 34698. 727-469-5942

LAKE MANATEE STATE PARK, 20007 Hwy 64 East, Bradenton, FL 34202. 941-741-3028

LITTLE MANATEE RIVER STATE PARK, 215 Lightfoot Road, Wimauma, FL 33598. 813-671-5005

Madeira Bickel Mound State Archeological Site, 3708 Patten Ave., Ellenton, Florida 34222. Tel: 941-723-4536

MYAKKA RIVER STATE PARK, 13208 S.R. 72, Sarasota, FL 34241. 941-361-6511

OSCAR SCHERER STATE PARK, 1843 S. Tamiami Trail, Osprey, FL 34229. 941-483-5956

Skyway Fishing Pier State Park, 4905 34th Street South #5000, St. Petersburg, Florida 33711. 727-865-0668

Stump Pass Beach State Park, Barrier Islands State Parks, P.O. Box 1150, Boca Grande, FL 33921. 941-964-0375

Ybor City Museum State Park, 1818 Ninth Ave., Tampa, FL 33605. 813-247-6323

Yulee Sugar Mill Ruins Historic State Park 3400 N. Museum Pointe Crystal River, FL 34428. Tel: 352-795-3817

TOURIST ATTRACTIONS

There are dozens of tourist attractions in Central West Florida. We will explore the following:

Dali Museum, St. Petersburg

Dinosaur World, Plant City

Crystal River Manatee Swim, Crystal River

Florida Aquarium, Tampa

Weeki Wachee Springs, Weeki Wachee

Dali Museum

1 Dali Boulevard
St. Petersburg, Florida 33701
Tel: 727-823-3767
Thedali.org

The Salvador Dali Museum is the home of the world's most comprehensive collection of the renowned Spanish artist's work.

Collected by **A. Reynolds Morse** and **Eleanor Morse** (close friends of Dali) over a 45-year period, it is celebrated for its **96 oil paintings**.

Art connoisseur or not, you will be enthralled by this St. Petersburg Florida tourist attraction which pays tribute to the czar of surrealism, Salvador Dali. It has become one of the most popular Florida tourist attractions.

Dali is best known for his dreamlike paintings in which he showed people and objects transformed into fantastic images that were often set in deserted landscapes.

Upon entering the Museum you find yourself confronted with Dali's work which can be a real "mind-bender". It's recommended you take a Guided Tour which informs you of the artist's work and what he was trying to convey. Half the fun is comparing your perception with that of the artist!

Florida's top-rated museum offers constantly changing exhibits that present a variety of activities including films, gallery talks and special exhibitions throughout the year. Like other Florida tourist attractions, the museum frequently changes what the public is going to see to keep interest at high levels.

Mom and Dad can introduce the kids to the world of avant-garde at the Museum on Saturdays from 11:45am - 4:30pm with "Dilly Dally with Dali", an enlightening program of games, puzzles, arts and crafts and activities.

Other programs include **"Breakfast with Dali"**, one Saturday a month from 9:00-11:00am, where children can take a tour followed by breakfast (fee and reservation required) and **"Coffee with a Curator"** the first Wednesday of each month with Starbucks Coffee followed by a tour at 10:15am with a Dali Museum Curator. This is free with paid admission.

While exploring the fascinating gift shop keep in mind Salvador Dali was a master of marketing. His merchandise is to be found nowhere else in the world. You can shop on-line by visiting the Dali store at the museum's website.

General Admission fee is $24 for adults, lower rates for children, teens and seniors (May 2016).

The Dali Museum in St. Petersburg Florida is open every day from 10:00am-5:30pm. On Thursday nights the Museum is open until 8pm.

Dinosaur World

Dinosaur World
5145 Harvey Tew Road
Plant City, Florida 33565
813-717-9865
Dinosaurworld.com

The entire family will go "prehistoric" as you explore this most unique of Florida tourist attractions set in a "Jurassic Park" atmosphere! Walk among 150 life-size dinosaur replicas including the notorious "T-Rex" as well as species you never knew existed. This small Florida tourist attraction mixes entertainment with education.

The kids will most likely be talking about this one even after they've visited the other better known Florida tourist attractions. For some unknown reason, most kids are crazy about dinosaurs. Maybe they know something we don't about these not obviously loveable creatures from the shadows of prehistory.

Dinosaur Walk is not the only attraction. There is also the Boneyard where you can uncover a life-size dinosaur skeleton. Near the Boneyard is the Fossil Dig where your family can play at being an archaeologist and their newest exhibit, Skeleton Garden with life-size dinosaur skeleton replicas. Other features include the Movie Cave where you can learn about dinosaurs in a subterranean setting, a museum, gift shop and children's playground.

When lunch time comes around the entire family will enjoy snacking with the dinosaurs in the Picnic Area. There is also a nice playground for the kids to enjoy.

Dinosaur World is open every day. This fun Florida tourist attraction is conveniently located at Exit 17 off I-4 near Plant City, between Orlando and Tampa.

At Exit 17, turn north onto Branch Forbes Road then take the first left onto Harvey Tew Road.

This world of dinosaurs is open every day from 900 AM - 500 PM December-January and 900 AM - 600 PM the rest of the year. Check their website for current admission fees.

Crystal River Manatees

I had my first swim with manatees many years ago at Merritt Island, Florida. As I was standing in the shallow water of the Indian River Lagoon scrubbing algae off the bottom of my boat, something huge and wet suddenly nudged me gently but firmly in the small of my back. I quickly turned around to look into the little button eyes of a manatee. He (or she) was about 10 feet long.

When my heart stopped pounding, I had fun stroking and petting him and giving him some water from the dock hose. My new friend and I slowly swam together around the marina. It was the first swim with manatees event at Jay's Harbor Lights Marina.

These days, swimming with manatees can be your vacation highlight. A swim with manatees these days is a whole lot more organized than was my spontaneous experience, especially at some of the Crystal River tourist attractions. Now you can go to Crystal River, 70 miles north of Tampa, and find numerous places that will take you to where the West Indian Manatees are.

Manatees are also known as sea cows. They can get to be 12 or 13 feet long and weigh 3000 pounds. These gentle mammals graze slowly in shallow waters munching sea grass like an aquatic cow. They also like to take naps down on the bottom.

They are usually very trusting, calm and curious. When you swim with manatees, you will be amazed at how safe they feel with you. Sad to say, but early Florida crackers and Caribbean natives took advantage of the manatee's trusting nature. They routinely killed these gentle creatures and got enough meat to live on for many months.

These days they are protected, but are still endangered by boats. They get killed or injured by boats crushing them between their hull and the bottom of the water body. The also get slashed badly by boat propellers.

Organizations like the **Save the Manatee Club** and individuals like singer/writer Jimmy Buffet are devoted to protecting the manatee.

The manatee's only big enemy is cold water. It will kill the animal, so it has to be very careful.

Manatees cannot survive in water below 60 degrees, so every winter in Florida they flock to where the warm water is. This is why cooling water discharges at **power plants** and **natural spring fed rivers** are always good manatee watching areas and informal Florida tourist attractions.

From **November through March**, Crystal River is the best place to swim with manatees or to watch them in Kings Bay. The headwaters of Crystal River, Kings Bay is fed by a number of fresh water springs that produce 600 million gallons daily at a consistent **72 degrees F** year round. Some people estimate that as many as 400 manatees take their winter vacation in the waters of Kings Bay.

There are many businesses in Crystal River that will take you snorkeling among the manatees. If you are lucky, you will see a baby manatee. They are so cute you will want to take one home with you. When you rub their belly they make little tiny chirping sounds like a baby chick. You will definitely see the large adult manatees. They will be very nonchalant around you. Neither you nor the manatee will feel threatened.

The town of Crystal River is home to about 3,600 people. It has all the lodging and restaurants you would expect of a town whose main industry is manatee based tourism. You have to love a town where City Hall is decorated with a red, white and blue manatee statue.

There are many businesses in Crystal River that offer swim packages. There are also kayak and canoe outfits that run manatee-sighting trips on the Crystal River and Kings Bay. Some of these outfits also run trips on the nearby Homosassa and Chassahowitzka Rivers.

Just a couple of these many businesses are as follows:

The American Pro Diving Center, 821 Southeast Highway 19; 352-563-0041; opens at 7 a.m. for the first Crystal River swim with manatees expedition of the day. The fee for the tour, including wet suite and snorkel gear is $69.50; the trip lasts three to four hours.

Crystal River Kayak Company, 1326 Southeast Highway 19; 352-795-2255; offers guided kayak and canoe tours of area bays and rivers, including a sunset paddle and a birding trip. Guided tours start at $50; kayak rentals start at $20 for three hours.

There is also a Florida State Park that offers manatee viewing tours:

Homosassa Springs Wildlife State Park, 4150 South Suncoast Boulevard, Homosassa Springs; 352-628-5343; is open every day from 9 a.m. to 5:30 p.m.; the ticket counter closes at 4 p.m., and the last boat ride to the park departs at 3 p.m. Tickets are $13 for adults and $5 for ages 6 to 12 (August 2015).

Florida Aquarium

701 Channelside Drive
Tampa, FL 33602
Tel: 813-273-4030
Flaquarium.org

Florida Aquarium is still known by many Floridians and tourists as the Tampa Aquarium. It is ranked in the top 10 aquariums in the United States by TripAdvisor and is ranked among the top 5 **"Kid-Friendly Aquariums"** by Parents Magazine. It is located in the heart of **Tampa** in a modern 200,000 square foot air conditioned building.

The aquarium is accredited by the Association of Zoos and Aquariums. It concentrates on teaching the visitor about the ecosystems of Florida and the rest of the world. The facility is more than an aquarium; it is also a botanical garden and aviary.

The aquarium has a creative way of telling about Florida's water resources and shows what happens to a single drop of water from its underground sources in the aquifers as it meanders its long way to the ocean.

The **water story** begins by showing birds and alligators and other animals in a Florida wetland. It then leads the visitor through the bays and beaches of Florida with its more than 20,000 plants and animals.

The aquarium also has interactive programs that teach about coral reefs, including "Swim With The Fishes", for non-certified divers, and **"Dive With The Sharks"** for certified divers.

In these programs a visitor can come eyeball to eyeball with a giant grouper or be very close to a penguin and other animals in exhibits with no barriers between the visitor and the animal, but in a safe manner. Another exhibit is **"Ocean Commotion"** where visitors can get up close to some very unusual marine animals like a clown fish and an octopus.

Certified **SCUBA** divers over the age of 15 can also get in the tank with sharks.

The aquarium has a 2 acre outside fun zone for kids with water cannons, high squirting geysers and a pirate ship. Behind the scenes tours are also offered where guests can see the machinery and operations that go into making the Tampa aquarium work. There are also exhibits that show the guest how to set up and maintain an aquarium at home.

The aquarium is open 7 days a week from 9:30 AM to 5:00 PM except for Thanksgiving and Christmas.

General Admission tickets are $24.95 for adults and less for children and seniors.

Weeki Wachee Springs

6131 Commercial Way
Spring Hill, Florida 34606
352-592-5656
Weekiwachee.com

Weeki Wachee Springs is one of those old Florida tourist attractions, like Marineland, that everybody wanted to visit in the 1950s and 1960s. After Walt Disney World opened in October 1971, attendance at Weeki Wachee Springs began to decline.

The photo above of the lovely young mermaids is from the State Archives of Florida, Florida Memory.

In its glory days, beautiful young women came from all over the world to audition for roles as mermaids. As many as 500,000 people a year flocked to see the mermaid shows. Famous people from Florida and elsewhere came to the springs. **Don Knotts, Elvis Presley** and **Esther Williams** are among the celebrities who visited or made films.

Some Florida towns offered local women jobs in factories or paper mills. Young ladies in Weeki Wachee, Brooksville, Spring Hill and other Central West Florida towns looked forward to getting a job as a mermaid. These ladies are a close knit bunch and reminiscent of the Marine Corps slogan, the motto of current and present performers is: **"Once A Mermaid, Always A Mermaid"**.

Today Weeki Wachee Springs is part of the Florida State Park system. This is good for the financial stability of the operation, and adds to the fun of the attraction. Mermaid shows are held again, and even former mermaids come back to swim in reunions.

Buccaneer Bay, a water slide attraction, opened in 1982, to compete with Wet N Wild in Orlando and other water attractions with flumes and waves. You will enjoy seeing the mermaids swim in the springs. It is one of the major events that have made this one of the most enduring Florida tourist attractions.

Once in a while they are joined by the natives of the springs: turtles, fish, manatees, otters and even an alligator now and then.

Visitors can swim in the springs (with the Sea Diver program), and have their pictures taken with the mermaids.

In addition to the fun at Buccaneer Bay and with the mermaids, canoes and kayaks are available to rent, along with inner tubes, to drift down the Weeki Wachee River. A river cruise is also available.

All in all, a fun couple of days can be spent at this most wonderful and laid back of Old Florida tourist attractions.

GENERAL ADMISSION FEES

Adults $13.00, Children $8.00 (May 2016)

HOURS

A word of caution about the hours of operation: Weeki Wachee Springs has a schedule that varies depending on the time of year. It also varies depending on whether Buccaneer Bay is open or closed.

I advise checking their website for current operating hours and days of operation, or call at 352-592-5656.

WINERIES

There are 4 Central West Florida wineries listed in this travel guide:

Florida Orange Groves, Inc., St. Petersburg

Keel and Curley Winery, Plant City

Rosa Fiorelli Winery Inc., Bradenton

Strong Tower Vineyard & Winery, Spring Hill

Central West Florida Travel Guide will give you detailed information about these wineries.

Florida Orange Groves

1500 Pasadena Ave S
South Pasadena, FL 33707
727-347-4025
Floridawine.com

Florida Orange Groves Winery is a family owned business located in the South Pasadena area of the busy St. Petersburg metropolitan region. The company got its start packing and shipping fresh citrus in the early 1970s.

They gradually grew the business over the years to include retail sales of fresh citrus juice and an associated gift shop. The family began developing their **unique wines made from citrus** in 1991, and opened the winery in 1997.

They now produce wines from key limes, mango, pink grapefruit and many other citrus fruits and berries. They are also one of the few Florida wines presented at Disney's **Epcot International Food and Wine Festival** held each year beginning in October.

Florida Orange Groves Winery currently produces 33 different types of wine.

All of their premium specialty tropical, berry and citrus wines are made 100% from the juice indicated on the label. These are not fusion or blended grape wines, but 100% pure tropical fruit wines. It can take upwards of nine pounds of fruit to produce one bottle of wine. Each individual variety of our wine tastes like the juice that it is made from.

They are set up so you can buy wine online, and also have a free wine tasting bar.

The gift shop is reminiscent of the old Stuckey roadside shops of years ago in the south, replete with souvenirs.

HOURS OF OPERATION

Monday - Saturday: 9:00am - 5:00pm
Sunday: 12:30pm - 5:00pm
Tours at 11:00am, 1:00pm, 2:00pm and 3:00pm

DIRECTIONS

From I-275 in St. Petersburg, take 22nd Ave S west for 1.3 mi to Gulfport Blvd S. Take Gulfport Blvd S for 2.6 mi to Pasadena Avenue South. Turn left on Pasadena Avenue South.

For more information about wines and events, call 727-347-4025.

Keel and Curley Winery

5210 W. Thonotosassa Road
Plant City, FL 33565
Phone: 813-752-9100
Keelandcurleywinery.com

Keel and Curley Winery is near Plant City about 15 miles east of downtown Tampa. The winery and its farm are located on 25 acres on Thonotosassa Road in east Hillsborough County. My friends do not believe me when I tell them that the road is named after Lake Thonotosassa, an Indian word that means **"lake on the shores of which we find flints to start our fires"**.

Joe Keel is a Floridian who has been growing blueberries in the area for years. Every year after harvest, his unsold blueberries were frozen. This is when the idea of blueberry wine came into his mind. Joe found a Vermonter, **Chase Marden**, and they partnered up. Chase had experience developing fruit wines in Burlington, Vermont. They bottled their first wine in 2003, and now produce 16 different varieties.

The blueberries are picked by hand, crushed, fermented and bottled right on the property. The blueberry wines come dry, semi-dry and sweet.

In addition to the blueberry wines, they also make fruit fusion wines. These include grape varieties fused with tropical fruits. They also have traditional grape wines made from California grapes.

Recently, the winery has added **Two Henrys Brewing Company**. They make hand crafted beer - also available for sale in the winery. They have a nice tasting room and gift shop. All of their wines can be purchased in the store. The building also has a nice big deck to enjoy the country air.

Keel and Curley Winery has a Happy Hour. **"UNCORKED"** is the winery's after hours wine bar. It's open every Friday and Saturday from 5:00 pm to midnight. **Happy Hour** is from 5:00 pm to 6:30 pm. You can enjoy live music along with your wine or craft beer.

The winery also has banquet facilities, and is the scene of many weddings and wedding parties. The beautiful gazebo is a perfect setting for the ceremony. The landscaped grounds, grape vineyard and spacious deck are ideal for a wedding reception. The winery advises calling well ahead to book your date, as popular dates are commonly booked a year in advance.

Unlike many Florida wineries, Keel and Curley Winery sells their wines at your friendly **Publix, Total Wine & More** and several other stores found throughout the State of Florida.

HOURS OF OPERATION

Retail Store Hours
Sunday - Thursday: 11:00am - 6:00pm. Friday and Saturday: 10:00am - Midnight

Uncorked Wine Bar Hours

Friday and Saturday: 5:00pm - 11:00pm

DIRECTIONS

From I-4, take Exit 17.

Turn left on Branch Forbes Road. It becomes North Branch Forbes Road.

Turn left on Thonotosassa Road (CR-580). You will see the winery at 5210 Thonotosassa Road.

Rosa Fiorelli Winery

4250 CR-675
Bradenton, FL 34211
941-322-0976
Fiorelliwinery.com

Rosa Fiorelli Winery is a family owned and operated business located east of Bradenton in the rolling hills south of Lake Manatee. Rosa Fiorelli and her husband Antonio moved here from Sicily. They were struck by the similarities with their country. They started growing grapes on their property, and began making wine in a corner of their garage.

From this modest start, they have grown to have a 10 acre vineyard and a 3,000 square foot winery.

Although they have only been in business since 1998, they have already won 100 awards in commercial international wine competition. They have gradually expanded to 10 acres of vineyard and a 3,000 square foot building for fermenting and bottling, and another building for retail sales and wine tasting.

Their wine selections include NV Rosato (a semi-dry rose), NV Aurora Muscadine White and NV Red Muscadine Dessert.

The winery offers free wine tastings every day from opening to closing.

HOURS OF OPERATION

Monday: 10:00am - 5:30pm
Wednesday - Saturday: 10:00am - 5:30pm
Closed Tuesdays and Holidays
Closed October 7 - October 14
DIRECTIONS

From I-75, take SR-64 east about 8 miles to CR-675. Turn right (south) on CR-675 and go less than one mile to the winery.

Strong Tower Vineyard and Winery

17810 Forge Drive
Brooksville, FL 34610
Tel: 352-799-7612
Strongtowervineyard.com

The **Strong Tower Vineyard & Winery** is visible from the **Suncoast Parkway** south of Spring Hill. It takes a little pleasant backroad travel to get there. The Parkway is a beautiful new toll road that runs north from Tampa to south of Homosassa. It makes this vineyard an easy visit from Tampa.

Terry and Janis McKnight own Strong Tower Vineyard & Winery, and grow four grape varieties on their property. These grapes include **Blanc du Bois, Norton**, and two **Muscadine** grapes named **Ison** and **Carlos**.

Each of these grapes has a unique quality that is reflected in the wine produced from them.

You will enjoy your walk to the vineyard when you visit. The vineyard is open for **"U-Pick"** in harvest season. This is fun to do, and the grapes are so delicious right off the vine. All of the wines are estate grown and produced. This means that from the beginning with the grapes in the vineyard to the finished labeled bottle, everything is done on the property.

Among the types of wine produced here are Whites, reds and blush wines ranging from dry to sweeter. These wines have won top awards in a recent eleven country International Wine Competition.

All of their wines are natural and low in sulphites.

Your visit will include a complimentary tasting in the winery and a tour of the processing room. The winery store carries wine accessories and gifts in addition to all of their wines. They can also accommodate private party tastings or other events like birthdays, anniversaries or music recitals. There is also a nice veranda where you can sit and enjoy your wine and the country view.

HOURS OF OPERATION

Wednesday - Saturday: 10:00am - 6:00pm
Closed Sunday - Tuesdays and Major Holidays

DIRECTIONS

From the Suncoast Parkway or Highway 19:

Take County Line Rd. (Exit 37 on the Suncoast Parkway). Go east to US-41, then south on 41 one mile to Bowman Rd. Then right (west) on Bowman until you come to Forge Drive. Left on Forge Dr. before the overpass.

Strong Tower is the first house you come to - park right in front, come right on in, they've been expecting you!

From Tampa:

Take I-75 north to SR-52 West. West to US-41 north, and north eight miles to Bowman Rd. Left (west) on Bowman. Left on Forge Dr. before the parkway overpass.

You can also travel from Tampa on the Suncoast Parkway (see above).

FESTIVALS

Central West Florida art festivals are held throughout the year in many towns and cities of the region including **St Petersburg, Tampa, Clearwater, Sarasota, Bradenton** and **Lakeland.** I have attended many festivals and art shows during my years in Florida and have enjoyed every one of them.

Here is a partial list of annual art festivals, craft shows, folk festivals and other outdoor events in Central West Florida arranged by month:

JANUARY

Third Weekend (Weekend before MLK Day)
Black Heritage Festival - Tampa

Fourth Weekend
Sarasota Masters Art Festival - Sarasota

FEBRUARY (No art shows reported.)

MARCH

First Weekend
Sanibel Shell Fair - Sanibel

Gasparilla Festival of the Arts - Downtown Tampa

Second Weekend
Annual Manatee Arts Festival- Apollo Beach

Last Weekend
Seafood Fest - Bradenton

Tarpon Springs Fine Arts Festival - Tarpon Springs

APRIL

Second Weekend
Celebration of the Art - Wesley Chapel

Third Weekend
Mainsail Arts Festival - St. Petersburg (Vinoy Park.

MAY

Fourth Weekend
Orange Blossom Jamboree - Brooksville

JUNE-OCTOBER (No art shows reported.)

NOVEMBER

First Weekend
Art Harvest - Dunedin

Venice Art Festival - Venice

DECEMBER

First Weekend
Sarasota Craft Show - Sarasota

Second Weekend
Winterfest - Anna Maria Island

HERITAGE AND HISTORY

Central West Florida heritage begins with the early Native Americans who dwelled in the area 12,000 years ago. The modern history of the region begins during the three Seminole Wars from 1816 to 1858 when forts and trails were established to support the wars

After these wars, the area began to be settled by southerners and other Floridians and ethnic groups. Tarpon Springs became a Greek enclave of sponge fishermen and their families. Tampa had large influxes of Cuban and Italian immigrants. The history of Tampa had a major influence on the region.

This heritage is shared by all the counties in Central West Florida. Each county has its fair share of sites that are an important part of Florida history. The Tampa Bay area is culturally diverse with historic communities of Cuban and Italian immigrants who have been Floridians for well over one hundred years.

The more rural areas are culturally southern with many settlers having been from Confederate families who moved down after the Civil War.

Central West Florida History

Florida history is full of articles about **Henry Flagler** and his extension of the Florida East Coast Railway from **St. Augustine** all the way down to **Key West**. **Henry Plant** is not as well known to Florida history, but he had a similar impact on the development in this other coast of Florida and he is an important part of Central West Florida heritage and history.

Tampa was a small fishing village on the Hillsborough River when Plant's railroad came to town in the 1880's. He built the **Tampa Bay Hotel** between 1888 and 1891. The hotel was designed to surpass all other grand winter resorts. At a cost of $3 million, the 511-room giant rose to a flamboyant height of five stories, surrounded by ornate Victorian gingerbread and topped by Moorish minarets, domes and cupolas.

During the Spanish American War, the U.S. Army used the facilities as a staging area for the invasion of Cuba. Among the soldiers who stayed there was future American president **Teddy Roosevelt** and his **Rough Riders**. Florida history and American history quite often intersect like this.

The Tampa Bay Hotel is now the home of the **University of Tampa** and the visible centerpiece of Central West Florida heritage.

In addition to Tampa, Central West Florida heritage and history includes the populated areas of **St. Petersburg, Clearwater** and **Sarasota**. This region of Florida has 8 counties, ranging from rural Desoto County to Hillsborough and Pinellas Counties. Some of these are the most rural and culturally southern areas remaining in the state.

It is also known as the western part of the **I-4 Corridor**. Tampa, Orlando and Daytona Beach are all growing toward each other along this corridor. Someday it will probably all resemble one big city just as south Florida does along I-95 from West Palm Beach to south of Miami.

Central West Florida is a very urban region with large populations in Tampa and St. Petersburg. With Busch Gardens in Tampa and with Orlando only an hour or less away, this area is also a rival to Miami and Orlando in the Florida tourism industry. Like Central Florida, the region also has vast agricultural operations. Groves and farms predominate in the eastern part of the region away from the coast.

Central West Florida heritage is culturally diverse. The northern and eastern counties are rural and more southern. **Brooksville** in rural **Hernando County** has a statue of a confederate soldier in front of the City Hall. **Cowboys** with Stetson hats and hand rolled cigarettes can still be found around town in **Arcadia**.

Tampa heritage has been influenced by the **Cuban cigar industry** that flourished here more than 100 years ago. **Ybor City,** named after Cuban cigar king **Vicente Martinez Ybor**, is a working neighborhood with fine lodging and restaurants.

The southern part of Central West Florida -**Sarasota, Bradenton** and **Venice** - is culturally more like the American Midwest than the rest of Florida. Cattle and farm fields sprawl across the landscape.

Before the interstate highways, US-41 fed transplants into west coast Florida from **Indiana, Michigan, Wisconsin, Ohio, Illinois** and **Minnesota**. Their New England counterparts took US-1 down the east coast to Palm Beach, Broward and Miami-Dade Counties.

My grandparents retired to Venice in 1962. They drove down US-41 from Indiana in their beat up 1953 Chevy BelAir. I guess my Hoosier grandparents were part of Florida history. I guess we all are because the State has changed so fast and most of us Floridians are from someplace else.

Until recent years, it was rare to hear a **New York** or **Boston** brogue in **Central West** or **Southwest Florida**. That all changed after the completion of I-75 and I-95. The completion of those major interstate highways made it easier for people up north to escape the snow and drive to either coast.

The New England brogue is now showing up in Central West Florida. The Midwestern twang is also now more common in East Central and Southeast Florida than before the new interstate highways. Florida has always been the melting pot of the United States. That is the Central West Florida heritage as well.

Fishing is a Central West Florida heritage that binds people together from all parts of the world. Each region of Florida has its own best fishing spots, both fresh and salt water. The beach communities west of St. Pete are staging points for a lot of great charter fishing.

Central West Florida Heritage Sites

Here is a list of 225 Central West Florida heritage sites listed by county. The County Seat is also listed.

CITRUS: Inverness

Crystal River Archaeological State Park
Crystal River Indian Mounds
Fort Cooper
Fort Cooper State Park
Historic Hernando School
Homosassa Springs Wildlife State Park
Museum of Citrus County History - Old City Hall
The Old Courthouse Heritage Museum
Withlacoochee Trail State Park
Yulee Sugar Mill Ruins
Yulee Sugar Mill Ruins Historic State Park

DESOTO: Arcadia

Arcadia Historic District

HERNANDO: Brooksville

May-Stringer Heritage Museum
South Brooksville Avenue Historic District

HILLSBOROUGH: Tampa

22nd Street South Redevelopment Corp.
Alafia River State Park
American Victory Mariners Memorial and Museum Ship
Bay Isle Commercial Building
Camp Bayou Nature Preserve

Centro Asturiano de Tampa

Cigar Maker's House Museum

Cracker Country at the Florida State Fairgrounds

Downtown Plant City Commercial District

Downtown Plant City Historic Residential District

Egmont Key State Park

El Centro Espanol of Tampa

El Circulo Cubano de Tampa

El Pasaje Building

Federal Building US Courthouse

Floridan Hotel

Fort Foster

Glover School Site

Grand Central District

Hampton Terrace Historic District

Hillsborough River State Park

Hillsborough State Bank Building

Historic Turkey Creek High School

Hutchinson House

Hyde Park Historic Districts

Kress Building

Little Manatee River State Park

Main Street Zephyrhills, Inc.

Masonic Temple # 25

North Franklin Street Historic District

North Plant City Residential District

Old Lutz Elementary School

Old Schoolhouse

Old Tampa Free Public Library

Old Union Depot Hotel

Pioneer Village Museum

Plant City High School Community Center

Plant City Union Depot
Plant Hall at University of Tampa
Quintilla Geer Bruton Archives Center
Ruskin Women's Club
Seminole Heights Residential District
St. James House of Prayer Episcopal Church
Standard Oil Service Station
Taliaferro House
Tampa Bay History Center
Tampa City Hall
Tampa Heights Historic District
Tampa Police Memorial
Tampa Theatre
Tampania House
Union Railroad Station
West Tampa Historic District
William E. Curtis House
Ybor City Historic District
Ybor City Main Street
Ybor City Museum State Park
Ybor Factory Building

MANATEE: Bradenton

Anna Maria Island Historical Museum
Beth Salem
Braden Castle Park Historic District
Bradenton Beach Scenic Highway
Bradenton Carnegie Library
Cortez Historic District
De Soto National Memorial
Family Heritage House
First Manatee County Courthouse

Florida Gulf Coast Railroad Museum, Inc.

Gamble Plantation Historic State Park

Lake Manatee State Park

Madeira Bickel Mound State Archaeological Site

Manatee Village Historic Park

Midway Subdivision Historic District

Palmetto Historic District

Portavant Temple Mound at Emerson Point Park

Robert Gamble House/ Judah P. Benjamin Confederate Memorial

Seagate

Shaw's Point Archaeological District

South Florida Museum

Whitfield Estates -- Broughton Street Historic District

Whitfield Estates Lantana Avenue Historic District

Women's Club of Palmetto

PASCO: Dade City

Amtrak Station

Baker House Museum

Church Street Historic District

Downtown Dade City Main Street

Greater New Port Richey Main Street, Inc.

Hacienda Hotel

Jeffries House

Pasco Fine Arts Council and Center

Pioneer Florida Museum and Village

St. Leo Abbey Historic District

Werner-Boyce Salt Springs State Park

West Pasco Historical Society Museum and Library

Zephyrhills Depot Museum

Zephyrhills Downtown Historic District

PINELLAS: Clearwater

Alexander Hotel
Anclote Key Lighthouse
Anclote Key State Park
Andrews Memorial Chapel
Arcade Hotel
Belleview-Biltmore Hotel
Boone House
Caladesi Island State Park
City Hall and Tarpon Springs Performing Arts Center
City Hall Annex
Clearwater Main Street Joint Venture
Cleveland Street Post Office
County Courthouse and Administration Building
Don Ce Sar Resort and Spa
Downtown Largo Main Steet Association
Duchess
Dunedin Historical Society
First United Methodist Church of St. Petersburg
Florida Holocaust Museum
Florida International Museum
Fort De Soto Batteries
George N. Cretekos
Green-Richman Arcade
Gulfport Historical Museum
Harbor Oaks Residential District
Historic Sunken Gardens
Honeymoon Island State Park
John C. Williams House
Johnson Building
Jungle Prada Mound Park
Kelly Hotel

Louis Ducros House

Moccasin Lake Nature Park

Mount Olive African Methodist Episcopalian Church

N.K. Symi

Old Belleair Town Hall

Old Palm Harbor Main Street

Old Tarpon Springs City Hall

Palm Harbor Historical Museum

Panama Canal Museum

Pass-a-Grille Historic District

Pinellas County Historical Museum

Renaissance Vinoy Resort

Roser Park Historic District

S.H. Kress and Co. Building

Safety Harbor Mound at Philippe Park

Safety Harbor Museum of Regional History

Safford House

Science Center of Pinellas County

Snell Arcade

South Ward School

St. Nicholas III

St. Nicholas VI

St. Petersburg High School

St. Petersburg Lawn Bowling Club

St. Petersburg Museum of History

St. Petersburg Public Library

St. Petersburg Woman's Club

Studebaker Building

Tarpon Springs Sponge Docks at Dodecanese Blvd

U.S. Open Air Post Office

Union Academy

Weedon Island Preserve

SARASOTA: Sarasota

African American Culture Center
American National Bank Building
Appleby Building
Armada Road Multi Family District
Bay Haven School of Basics Plus
Bee Ridge Woman's Club
Belle Haven Executive Suites
Blackburn Point Bridge
Burns Court Historic District
Ca' d'Zan - John and Mable Ringling Museum of Art
Caples'-Ringlings' Estates Historic District
Christy Payne Mansion
City Waterworks
Colson School of Art
Crisp Building
Crowley Museum and Nature Center
DeMarcay Hotel
Dr. C.B. Wilson House
Eagle Point Historic District
Edgewood Historic District
El Patio Hotel
F.A. DeCanizares House
Florida Studio Theatre
H.B. William House
Harding Circle Historic District
Historic Spanish Point
Indian Mound Park
Johnson Chapel Missionary Baptist Church
Johnson Schoolcraft Building
Lemon Bay Woman's Club
Myakka Schoolhouse

Municipal Auditorium - Recreation Club
Myakka River State Park
Oscar Scherer State Park
Osprey Archaeological and Historic Site
Osprey School
Phillippi Estate Park
Rigby's La Plaza Historic District
S.H. Kress Building
Sarasota County Courthouse
Sarasota Herald Building
Sarasota High School
Sarasota Opera House
Sarasota Times Building
Southside Elementary School
U.S. Post Office - Federal Building
Venezia Park Historic District
Venice Archives and Area Historical Collection
Venice Main Street, Inc.
Warm Mineral Springs
Worth's Block

DAY TRIPS AND SCENIC DRIVES

The Central West Florida day trips recommended in this guide are often staged on the back roads around Tampa and designed to keep you out of heavy urban traffic.

I-4 is the east-west interstate highway in this region, and traverses the width of the state of Florida from Daytona Beach through Orlando to Tampa. This urbanized area is known as the **I-4 Corridor**.

I-75 is the north-south interstate, and enters Florida near Jasper and meanders down the center of the state until it starts veering west toward Tampa. I-75 goes all the way to Miami.

The Suncoast Parkway is a north-south toll road that starts in Tampa near the airport and terminates on US-98 north of Brooksville.

The I-4 and I-75 exits are crowded with gas stations, restaurants and motels. You can travel the state quickly and easily on these highways (except during rush hours), but not see as much scenery or real towns as on our recommended Central West Florida day trips.

The town signs you do see are usually a few miles from the downtown section. The fun begins when you get off the interstate and hookup with the less traveled roads that go through smaller Florida towns. There are many state and county highways off the interstate that offer better scenery and a look at real towns. In Florida, some backroads are even four-laned.

The maps below show the routes of a few Central West Florida day trips that I recommend.

Bushnell to Floral City

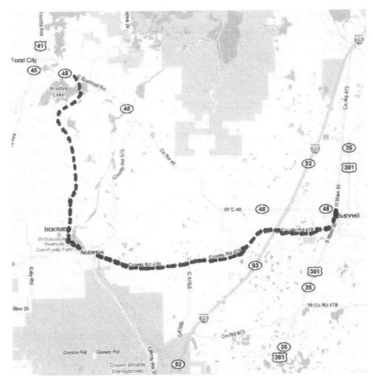

SR-476 from Bushnell west to Nobleton. Then north on SR-39 to Floral City, through Istachatta and Juneau. Peaceful country, parallels the rails to trails project, the Withlacoochee Trail. About 24 miles.

Inverness to Crystal River

Sr-44 from Inverness to Crystal River through Lecanto. Pretty hills and lake views. About 18 miles.

Weeki Wachee to Hudson

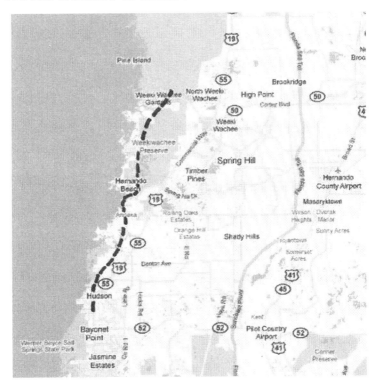

SR-595 from SR-50 just west of Weeki Wachee south to Hudson, through Hernando Beach and Aripeka. Low country, fishing villages, marshes, houses on stilts. About 18 miles.

Holiday to Dunedin

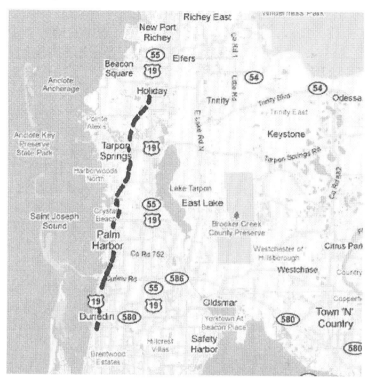

SR-595 aka Alternate US-19 from Holiday south to Clearwater through Tarpon Springs, Palm Harbor, Ozona and Dunedin. These are old Florida towns with a lot of interesting houses and plenty of trees. About 18 miles.

Tampa Day Trips

The Tampa Florida day trips and one day trips presented on this website are all within 100 miles of Tampa. The average car can get at least 250 miles on a tank of gas. Some compact cars can get quite a bit more. The Tampa Florida day trips described below can be made with gallons to spare for sightseeing and back road exploring on the trip.

Here are some things to do and places to see from Tampa. The map below shows you some of the major cities and places within a 100 mile radius of Tampa. Although many of the places are in Central West Florida, others are in Central Florida and Southwest Florida.

Recommended Tampa Florida Day Trips

Alva is a small town on the Caloosahatchee River west of Fort Myers. It has a small museum and an Old Florida ambiance with lots of oaks and Spanish moss and the lazy river flowing by. It was not named for Thomas Alva Edison, but for a Danish flower.

Arcadia has an annual rodeo and is in the heart of cattle country. Downtown has been restored and a couple of nice bed and breakfasts and antique stores make this a good weekend getaway.

Babcock Wilderness Adventures near Punta Gorda takes you on a tour of a working Florida ranch. You not only see the operation, but get to ride through one of Florida's most pristine natural settings.

Boca Grande is on the south end of Gasparilla Island and has the laid back charm of an end of the road village. Good relaxing, good dining, great beaches.

Bok Tower Gardens is a peaceful retreat near Lake Wales. A carillon tower and lush landscaping mark this National historic treasure.

Bradenton is a small city south of Tampa Bay that has great arts, seafood and beaches. It is the little brother to nearby Sarasota.

Brooksville is in rolling hill and spreading oak country. An old southern town with a Confederate soldier statue standing guard over its county courthouse.

Captiva Island has some of the finest shelling beaches in the world. Just north of Sanibel, it is a great place to relax for a day, week or lifetime.

Crystal River Swim with Manatees is a fun family activity where various tour operators provide the equipment and let you swim among manatees in the super clear waters in this area north of Tampa.

Dali Museum in downtown St. Petersburg has the world's largest permanent exhibit of the works of this great master. The architecture of the building is also a work of art.

Dinosaur World near Plant City is an attraction that the entire family will enjoy, especially the kids. Your kids will thank you for making this one of your Tampa Florida day trips.

Edison and Ford Winter Estates in Fort Myers are the well preserved winter homes of Thomas Alva Edison and Henry Ford. Edison's laboratory is an interesting well preserved attraction.

Englewood is a town on the beach that is a delight to visit. It is off the beaten path on the way to Boca Grande. Nice shops and restaurants, great beaches.

Florida Aquarium in downtown Tampa is one of the largest and finest in the world. It is also known as the Tampa Aquarium. For kids, this will be one of the most popular Tampa Florida day trips.

Florida Orange Groves is an historic winery in St. Petersburg. You can see how wine is made and do some sampling.

Fort Desoto Park has one of the finest beaches in Florida. It is located south of St. Petersburg in Tierra Verde. The trip to the beach is a very scenic drive.

Fort Meade is a small historic town established on the site of a fort used during the Seminole Wars.

Fort Myers is the major city in southwest Florida and is an easy trip from Tampa. Lots of great boating, the huge nearby community of Cape Coral, not far from Naples.

Keel and Curley Winery in Plant City is a family owned vineyard that specializes in blueberry wines. Nice bar and **tastings.**

Lakeland is a beautiful mid-sized city between Tampa and Orlando on I-4. It has many downtown lakes, and the Frank Lloyd Wright designed campus of Florida Southern College.

Naples and Old Naples are gems of the southwest coast. Lots of culture, dining, shopping, a great zoo and botanical garden and world class beaches.

Oscar Scherer State Park is in the Venice, Florida area. It is a full service park with lots of things to do during the day and some beautiful camp sites.

Punta Gorda is a small town on the southern shore of Peace River and Charlotte Harbor. Some of the best sailing in Florida, good shopping and dining.

Rosa Fiorello Winery near Bradenton is a family owned enterprise. Enjoy watching the wine making process and sampling the wares.

Sarasota has a beautiful waterfront setting and great beaches. It has some of the finest are exhibits and museums in Florida. Home of New College and the John and Mabel Ringling residence.

St. Petersburg has a beautiful downtown area that has been restored and is a vital center for shopping and dining. Private and city marinas line the waterfront, and the Vinoy Renaissance hotel is on the National Register of Historic Places.

Strong Tower Vineyard and Winery is a small family owned business near Spring Hill and Brooksville. You will see how the grapes are grown, the wine made, and can sample the products.

Tampa itself can keep you busy for days with Florida Aquarium, Lowry Park Zoo, Ybor City, Columbia Restaurant, professional football and waterfront everywhere you look. Although your Tampa Florida day trips start here, don't forget to visit as much as you can here too.

Venice is a small town with great beaches on the Gulf and a downtown area that is loaded with antique shops and good restaurants. The beaches offer the best shelling in Florida.

Webster has the biggest flea markets in Florida, but they only open on Mondays.

Weeki Wachee Springs is not only a beautiful state park, it is a popular attraction with mermaid shows that goes back many years into Old Florida history.

Winter Haven, a pretty town among the lakes The home of LEGOLAND on the grounds of the former Cypress Gardens.

EPILOGUE

Mike Miller has lived in Florida since 1960. He graduated from the University of Florida with a degree in civil engineering and has lived and worked in most areas of Florida. His projects include Walt Disney World, EPCOT, Universal Studios and hundreds of commercial, municipal and residential developments all over the state.

During that time, Mike developed an understanding and love of Old Florida that is reflected in the pages of his website, **Florida-Backroads-Travel.com**. The website contains several hundred pages about places in Florida and things to do. The information on the website is organized into the eight geographical regions of the state.

Central West Florida Backroads Travel is based on the website. It is one of eight regional guides that can be downloaded in PDF format or purchased as Amazon Kindle or soft cover books. If you find any inaccuracies in this guide, including restaurants or attractions that have closed, please contact Mike at Florida-

Backroads-Travel.com and let him know. It is his intention to update the guide periodically and publish updated editions.

If you have enjoyed this book and read it on Amazon Kindle, Mike would appreciate it if you would take a couple of minutes to post a short review at Amazon. Thoughtful reviews help other customers make better buying choices. He reads all of his reviews personally, and each one helps him write better books in the future. Thanks for your support!

BOOKS BY MIKE MILLER

Florida Backroads Travel
Northwest Florida Backroads Travel
North Central Florida Backroads Travel
Northeast Florida Backroads Travel
Central East Florida Backroads Travel
Central Florida Backroads Travel
Central West Florida Backroads Travel
Southwest Florida Backroads Travel
Southeast Florida Backroads Travel
Florida Heritage Travel Volume I
Florida Heritage Travel Volume 2
Florida Heritage Travel Volume 3
Florida Wineries
Florida Carpenter Gothic Churches
Florida Festivals
Florida Everglades
Florida One Tank Trips Volume i
Florida Authors: Gone But Not Forgotten

Made in the USA
Middletown, DE
28 August 2021

47054286R10064